Be a Star Learner
with Little Bear & friends

TOP THAT

Licensed exclusively to Top That Publishing Ltd
Tide Mill Way, Woodbridge, Suffolk, IP12 1AP, UK
www.topthatpublishing.com
Copyright © 2015 Tide Mill Media
0 2 4 6 8 9 7 5 3 1
Manufactured in China

Little Bear is giving his friends a ride in his trailer.
Practise saying the words on this scene. Start with bee!

b is for bee

g is for goose

Little Bear's tractor is red.
Can you finish colouring it?

The leaves on the trees
are green. Trace the letters ...

green

† is for tractor

W is for wheel

What shape are the tractor wheels?

circle   square   oval

Tick the right answer

A friendly bird is watching
Little Bear. Trace the letters ...

bird

Little Bear and Tiny Bear are playing I spy in the jungle with their friend, Toucan.

l is for leaf

t is for tree

The bananas are yellow. Can you finish colouring them all?

The pineapples are yellow too. Trace the letters ...

f is for **flower**

How many pink flowers can you see?

Write the number here.

Who does this shape belong to? Colour it to match the one in the scene.

It's a warm, sunny day and Little Bear is on the beach.

h is for hat

n is for net

s is for sand

Little Bear has a big bucket.
Colour it blue to match the sea.

Find these stickers to complete the seaside scene ...

 1 bright yellow sun  2 seagulls 1 lighthouse

S is for sea

How many clouds are in the sky?

Write the number here.

11 •1

9 • •10 2• •3 Join the dots to draw the shape.

•8 6 4• Find it in the picture.

•7 •5 picture.

Tiny Bear is visiting her woodland friends today.
Who's missing?

r is for
rabbit

Can you find ...

1 little owl

1 green frog

1 little mouse

b is for butterfly

w is for water

How many toadstools can you count?

Write the number here.

Who does this shape belong to? Colour it to match the one in the scene.

Little Bear is building a sandcastle.
Can you help him by joining the dots?

c is for cloud

b is for blanket

The octopus has 8 purple legs.
Can you colour his body too?

Find 2 pink shells
and 3 orange shells.

He will need ...

 1 bucket

 1 spade

Colour the sandcastle yellow.

p is for pebbles

How many shells can you count altogether?

Write the number here.

Little Bear is snorkelling in the blue sea.
Finish colouring this underwater scene.

fl is for flipper

How many pebbles can
Little Bear see?

Write the number here.

The big sea plant is pink.
Trace the letters ...

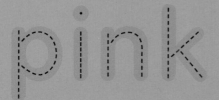

sh is for shell

 Can you spot this shape in the picture, then colour it to match?

The water is full of bubbles. Trace the letters ...

bubbles

You have to get up early when you work on a farm!

r is for roof

d is for door

What shape are the farmhouse windows?
triangle square diamond

Tick the right answer.

W is for window

Join the dots to finish
Little Bear's dungarees.
Then colour them blue.

Little Bear is going to collect eggs.
Trace the word ...

Little Bear is helping out with the chores at the stables.

What letter does this animal begin with?

d is for duck

How many animals can you count altogether?

Write the number here.

Colour the leaves on the tree.

Can you help him find ...

1 red wheelbarrow

1 big broom

b is for bird

c is for cat

Who does this shape belong to? Colour it to match the one in the scene.

The horse is peeping out of the stable. Trace the letters ...

horse

Next, Little Bear helps the farmer to feed and clean the pigs.

g is for goat

v is for vegetables

Can you find these shapes in the scene, then colour them to match?

He needs ...

 1 sack of vegetables  1 food trough 3 bales of hay

p is for pig

How many red things
can you see?

Write the number here.

Pigs love rolling in mud.
Trace the letters ...

mud

Rowing in the river is lots of fun!
Who is making bubbles in the water?

b is for boat

r is for river

How many fish can you count?

Write the number here.

What shape are the crocodile's teeth?

diamond triangle circle

Tick the right answer.

Find the fish that matches this shape, then make this one the same colour.

The blue snake says 'hiss'. Trace the letters then make the sound ...

hiss

Swordfish is swimming through a beautiful coral garden.

cl is for clam

Finish colouring Swordfish.
Which colour will you choose?

What shape are all the bubbles?

oval   circle   square

Tick the right answer.

Complete the scene with ...

   3 happy clams

1 hermit crab

Hermit Crab lives in a shell.
Trace the letters ...

If 1 clam went away,
how many would be left?

Write the number here.

Octopus is having a party today and all of his friends are invited.

S is for seaweed

Jellyfish has long tentacles.
Colour them blue, like his body.

Octopus looks very happy.
Trace the letters ...

octopus

j is for jellyfish

Who is hiding behind Octopus?

O is for octopus

Find the starfish shapes and colour them in. How many can you see?

Write the number here.

What colour is the seaweed?

green   yellow   red

Tick the right answer.

Tiny Bear is climbing a tree when she spots three of her friends.

t is for tiny twig

b is for big branch

Colour all the leaves on the big oak tree.

Squirrel loves acorns more than anything. Trace the letters ...

squirrel

Can you add them to the scene?

 1 blue bird

 1 red squirrel

 1 green frog

Squirrel only has 1 acorn. Colour in more, so she has 4 altogether.

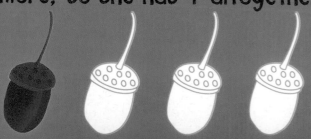

What colour are the dots on Little Bear's dress?

red   blue   white

Tick the right answer.

Angelfish is playing tag with her friends.

a is for anemone

S is for sea urchin

Angelfish has orange and yellow stripes. Finish colouring her in.

5 pink fish. 4 swim away. How many are left?

Can you find ...

5 pink fish

a is for angelfish

Little Bear and Tiny Bear are on safari!

S is for sunset

What shape is the hut's roof?

square diamond triangle

Tick the right answer.

Colour the sun in bright orange.

Add these animals to the scene and a place for them to stay ...

 1 grey elephant 1 purple snake 1 beach hut

h is for hill

Who does this shape belong to? Colour it to match the one in the scene.

It's fun to go on holiday! Trace the letters ...

holiday

Tiny Bear is watching her friends in secret.
Colour in this woodland scene.

Add 2 more birds.

What a busy springtime scene!
Add colour to bring it to life.

How many eggs are in the nest?

Can you spot the hiding bug?

Little Polar Bear is having fun in the snow.
Colour in this wintry scene.

Draw more snowflakes.

Add a snowman to the scene.

This underwater scene is full of fish and seaweed.
Can you make it look colourful?

How many seahorses can you see?

Add two starfish.

Little Bear is wondering what to do first.
Colour in the scene for seaside fun.

Colour the bucket in blue.

Colour the flippers in orange.

It's time for a jungle adventure!
Colour this scene to bring it to life.

Who is hiding in the water?

Add a big sun in the sky.

How many fish are
in the water?

Add 3 more fish.
How many fish are there now?

It's time to harvest the corn.
Colour in the busy summer scene.

Add 4 more bees in the sky.

Draw one more cloud.

Little Bear helps to gather the corn.
Add colour to finish the scene.

Colour the berries in purple.

Remember to make
the corn yellow!

Tiny Kitty loves jumping on the trampoline.
Colour the scene for bouncy fun!

Add more stars.

Give Tiny Kitty a red
top and green shorts.

Little Pup is doing his exercises.
Colour the scene for fitness fun!

How many weights does
Little Pup have?

Use a different colour
for each weight.

Little Rabbit is riding to her friend's house.
Colour the scene so she has a pretty view.

What shape are the wheels on
Little Rabbit's bicycle?

Colour Little Rabbit's top
in yellow.

Here are all the letters of the alphabet.
Can you trace each letter?

a b c d

i j k l

q r s t

y z

e f g h

m n o p

u v w x

Here are the numbers 1 to 10.
Can you trace each number, then count the animals?

6

7

8

9

10

Can you choose the right colour to fill in each shape?

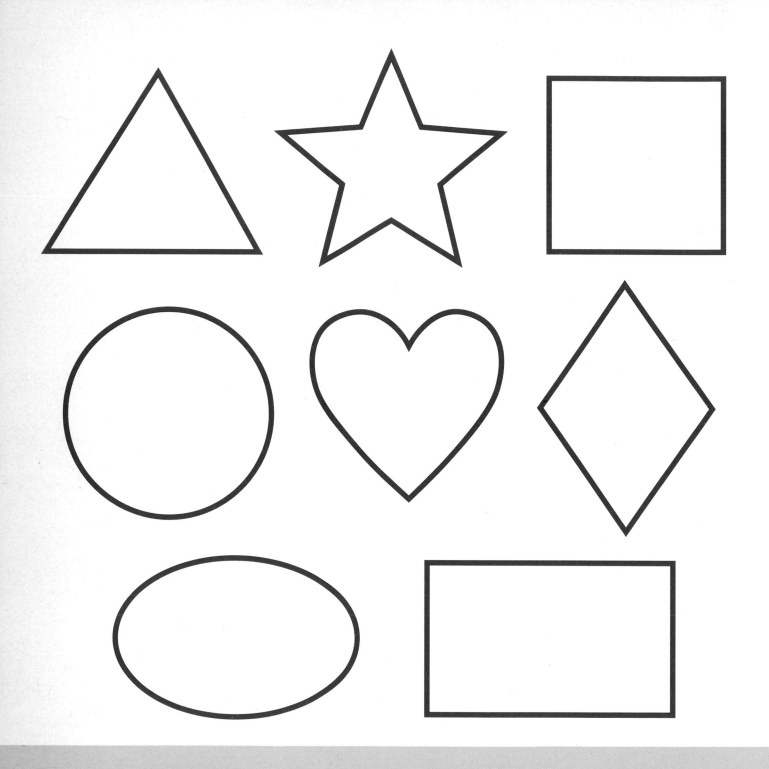

blue circle

red square

orange triangle

pink star

yellow oval

purple heart

black rectangle

green diamond